Mountain Rail and Locomotives from old Picture Postcards

by

Keith Taylorson

Plateway Press
ISBN 1 871980 39 9

Cover concept and book design by Keith Taylorson

Printed in Great Britain by Postprint, East Harling, Norfolk

ISBN 1 871980 39 9

Front cover illustration:
A turn of the century scene as a train prepares to leave Vitznau, Switzerland, on Nicholas
Riggenbach's pioneering rack and pinion railway to Rigi summit.

Back cover illustration:
No. 1 of the Achenseebahn, Austria, built by Vienna Locomotive Works, Floridsdorf in 1889,
receives attention at Jenbach.

Frontispiece:
The 3815m high mountain peak of the Aiguille du Dru dwarfs a descending train on the
Chamonix-Montenvers rack line, France.

CONTENTS

PREFACE

My two earlier books "Narrow Gauge and Miniature Railways from old Picture Postcards" (1986) and "Welsh Narrow Gauge Railways from old Picture Postcards" (1991)[1] explored the diverse world of the narrow gauge railway, using the medium of old postcards, published from around 1896 to the present day. Both volumes included some illustrations of mountain railways, however space considerations ruled out more than a representative coverage, and, by definition, standard gauge railways were excluded entirely. The author's collection of railway postcards having now grown to include over 200 examples featuring mountain railways, it was felt that a further volume concentrating entirely on this topic would be welcomed by many readers; all the more so, perhaps, as the only major English-language work on mountain railways is long out of print, and extremely scarce. While in no way seeking to emulate or supplant Schneider's erudite work, I hope that my illustrations and supporting text will serve to give the researcher, modeller and railway traveller a basic appreciation of this fascinating subject. A Bibliography is provided for those wishing to study the subject in more depth.

No attempt has been made to illustrate every mountain railway in the world. This would be impossible given the self imposed limitations of the subject, as some railways have never been depicted on postcards, others have, but problems of availability, picture quality or Copyright permission prevent their inclusion. For example, coverage of the famous Rimutaka incline in New Zealand has been rendered impracticable by the dearth of good quality postcards. Purposely omitted however is South America, whose mountain lines receive extensive coverage in another Plateway Press volume "Railways of the Andes."

As in the two previous volumes, the illustrations are drawn entirely from picture postcards. The majority are 'commercial' cards, produced by commercial publishers, as just one part of their output. 'Official' cards are those published by the railway company themselves, primarily for publicity purposes, though the profit motive may not be entirely absent. Finally there are photographic postcards, produced in small runs by individual photographers, primarily intended for collection rather than postal communication. Details of publishers are given in the captions, where known, though I have been defeated in some instances where the publisher's name is unclear, or omitted entirely. Within the main part of the book, most 'Golden Age' postcards have been reproduced exact size, but it has been necessary to reduce slightly those published to the larger 'Continental' format.

As regards basic data I have drawn heavily on Schneider[2] – other published sources consulted are listed in the Bibliography. The description of rack railway systems is adapted from an article in "Railway Wonders of the World," published around World War 1, but still a mine of information on the eclectic and obscure aspects of our railway world.

I am grateful to D. Trevor Rowe and to Lyndon Rowe for allowing me access to their postcard archives, to fill in gaps in my own collection. Trevor Rowe also provided valuable assistance in the compilation of a number of captions. Assistance was also provided by (in alphabetical order): Peter Arnold; Keith Chester; W. J. K. Davies; A. E. 'Dusty' Durrant; L. King; J. H. Price; Terry van Winkle; – to all of whom my grateful thanks are extended.

Brighton

[1] Written jointly with Andrew Neale; both these titles are currently (September 1999) out of print.
[2] Railways Through the Mountains of Europe by Ascanio Schneider.

INTRODUCTION

It is no surprise that railway development came later to mountainous areas than to other parts of the world's surface. Not only was commercial traffic less forthcoming, but the difficulties in driving rails through such hostile terrain, with the technology available in the 1830's, were overwhelming. For a while it was authoritatively (though as it turned out, quite wrongly) held that adhesion railways were impossible on gradients steeper than 1 in 100 (1 per cent), and this automatically ruled out extension of conventional railways to places thoughtless enough to be located in, on or behind mountains.

However the blossoming of knowledge, and the rapid advances in technology that occurred as the Railway Era got into its stride, made progress inevitable, and very soon minds were being turned towards the challenge of conquering the mountains, in the same way that deserts, forests and rivers were all being tamed by the iron road. Initially, cable haulage was used to cover short gaps judged too steep for adhesion working; but this was slow, expensive and inherently hazardous.[1] Before long inprovements in locomotive design made it possible to tackle gradients as steep as 1 in 40 ($2^1/_2$ per cent). This opened up the possibility of entirely adhesion routes across mountain ranges, ingenuity being applied to ways of crossing the mountain without exceeding the specified maximum grade.

6367 Bern-Lötschberg-Simplon

i) A powerful Brown Boveri locomotive heads a short train on the standard gauge Bern Lötschberg Simplon Railway (Switzerland), circa 1920.   *(b/w printed card, Phototypie Co., Neuchatel)*

ii) The metre gauge Bernina Bahn which connects Chur (Switzerland) with Tirano (Italy) via a summit at 2256m.

(b/w photographic card, Photoglob-Wehrli, Zurich)

iii) Carmel Viaduct on the breathtaking tramway line that once ran inland from Menton (France) to Sospel.

(coloured card, Edition Giletta)

Ways in which this was done include the reversing stub, and double reversing stub (otherwise known as zig-zag), extensively used in South America – these require the train to see-saw backwards and forwards onto successively higher sections of sloping track. In Europe, zig-zags were rare, being regarded as an operating inconvenience. Here the preferred method of gaining (or losing) height is the single or double loop, which does not require the train to stop or reverse, but which often involves the crossing and re-crossing of valleys by bridge or viaduct. Rarest of all is the spiral, by which the railway turns a full 360°, generally only practicable in wide open valleys – though the Swiss, with their supreme confidence and panache, confounded this wisdom by constructing many of theirs inside tunnels.[2]

Surprisingly, true pioneers in mountain railway construction in Europe were not the Swiss but the Austrians. Then a rich and powerful nation, the Austro-Hungarian Empire was hemmed in by mountains, but questions of economic and strategic interest, not to mention national pride, demanded that routes be driven through these obstacles at an early date. Plans for the Semmering route were launched as early as 1841, work actually commenced in 1848, and the line was opened throughout in 1854. Only shortly behind was the Brenner railway, connecting Innsbruck with Bozen (Bolzano), opened in 1858.

Another significant early mountain railway, the Mont Cenis line, connecting the railway networks of Italy and France, and which crossed the pass at a summit 2283 metres above sea level, was begun in 1860 and completed in 1871. Driving of the 12,219m. long tunnel used the then revolutionary pneumatic drills and took ten years to complete.

iii) Summit station on the Pike's Peak cog railroad, USA, circa 1901

(coloured card, Detroit Photographic Co.)

Switzerland – not the rich nation she is today, and with far more formidable barriers to development – had to proceed more slowly. The Gotthard line (Lucerne – Chiasso) which included the 1500m tunnel of the same name, took 20 years to build, and opened in 1882. Other major routes such as the Simplon and Lotschberg had to wait until 1905 and 1913 respectively before the completion of even longer tunnels made it possible to open them as through routes. Most of Switzerland's well known secondary routes, such as the Rhätische Bahn, Furka-Oberalp and Berninabahn, date from the first two decades of this century.

Construction of these through and later secondary routes involved the injection of massive amounts of capital, huge inputs of manpower and material, but relatively little technical innovation. Infinitely more challenging was the task of ascending the mountains themselves, to open up the slopes and summits to the burgeoning tourist market. These problems were being addressed by engineers in various parts of the globe, a number of viable systems eventually emerging – including the Fell system, Riggenbach's rack and pinion, and the Abt rack (see Conquest of the Clouds, page 9).

In contrast to the depressing pattern of closure and rationalisation that has affected the railways featured in our earlier two books, the passage of time has treated the mountain railway more kindly. This is mainly due to their traversing terrain as hostile to the building of roads as it was to the construction of railways. Thus road transport has not been an effective competitor, and the majority of railways featured in this book still survive, albeit few in totally unaltered form, and – except for a handful of rack lines in tourist areas – steam traction is now a thing of the past.

v) A loaded train climbing out of Monte Carlo on the short-lived rack line to La Turbie.

(coloured card, Levy Fils et Cie.)

---

[1] Despite which, isolated examples of cable haulage remained in use into the present Century, the last significant example – on the Langreo Railway in Spain – ceasing operation as late as 1969.

[2] By way of demonstrating that the oldest solution is often the best applicable to a modern problem, the Ffestiniog Railway in Wales built a brand new spiral in the 1970's, when forced to re-route its line above an encroaching reservoir.

CONQUEST OF THE CLOUDS
Rack Railway Systems and their Locomotives

There are definite limits to the climbing powers of any conventional type of locomotive. When the gradient becomes too steep the adhesion becomes insufficent to move the train, and the wheels 'spin' idly on the rails. Whenever possible, therefore, mountain railways are built with wide sweeping curves or spiral tunnels to gain height. Often, however, the engineer has no alternative but to scale the mountain-side by a direct route. Then some means of increasing the adhesion between engine and rails becomes essential.

The most common form of mountain-climbing device is the rack or toothed rail, with which there engages a power-driven pinion wheel on the engine. The rack and pinion for railway work was patented by John Blenkinsop in 1811, and was adopted on the lines of the Middleton, Kenton and Coxlodge Collieries in 1812-13. These colliery lines were not, of course, mountain railways, and Blenkinsop's idea was to enable a lightweight engine to haul a greater load than had been found possible with a heavy engine having smooth wheels.

Following on Blenkinsop's invention, patents were granted in 1824 to a Mr Snowden for a rack rail that in mechanical principles had a counterpart in the Locker system used on the Pilatus railway in Switzerland over sixty years later. Snowden suggested the use of a pair of flat-topped rails, one of which was to have a rack on its inner side, the teeth lying horizontally. A hollow rail of U-section was to be laid midway between the running rails.

The wagon was to have flangeless wheels. To keep it on the track rollers were fitted at either end, to run in the central hollow rail. To propel the wagon a toothed wheel on the lower end of a vertical shaft engaged with the rack. To the upper end of the shaft was to be fitted a capstan. Snowden's vision was to get rid of the steam locomotive altogether, and he envisaged this capstan being turned by four men, who would wind the wagon to the top of an incline, then presumably dodge clear of the capstan bars on the downhill journey. To the profound relief of generations of locospotters, Snowden's scheme was never put into practice.

In 1836 a rack locomotive was built at the Neath Abbey works in South Wales for the Dowlais Ironworks. This engine had two cylinders driving the rear wheels together with a pinion wheel gearing with a rack laid between the rails. The pinion wheel could be lifted up on level stretches of line not provided with a rack. Two years later the Neath Abbey works built a particularly interesting rack engine for the Rhymney Iron Company. This locomotive was probably one of the earliest articulated engines, and was carried on two four-wheeled trucks coupled together under the boiler. The trucks were provided with toothed wheels gearing with the rack and driven by a pair of outside cylinders through an auxiliary shaft. The teeth of the pinion were rounded to allow the articulated trucks to negotiate sharp curves.

At Madison, U.S.A., two Baldwin locomotives were put in service for operating a stretch of rack line in 1848. These engines had eight-coupled wheels driven by outside cylinders. The pinion was driven by a separate pair of cylinders placed vertically on the boiler. The pinion could be raised if required by means of a special steam cylinder.

Credit for the earliest successful application of rack technology to a true mountain railway must go to Sylvester Marsh, promoter of the Mount Washington Cog Railroad in the U.S.A., which opened in 1867. Marsh's device (patented 1863) for making the locomotive safe, either while ascending or descending a grade, involved a method for applying the power to the rear axle by means of cog gears. The other device was a ratchet arrangement which could be used to engage the cog wheel at once, should the steam power fail, and in this way prevent the train from running downhill.

Locomotives servant pour le train à crémaillère

F CF F

vi) No. 1 of the CF a Crémaillère de Langres, France was designed by Riggenbach himself and was built at Belfort in 1887, the year of the line's opening. The relative simplicity of the moving parts of the Riggenbach type locos is well shown in this view. *(b/w printed card, Lucien Levy)*

vii) 99.7305 is a metre gauge 0-4-2T from Krauss Linz, one of five supplied to work the Abt rack line from Puchberg to Hochschneeburg, Austria. The more complex system of cranks and connecting rods customary on the Abt type of locomotive is readily apparent. *(b/w photographic, Locomotivbild-Archiv)*

In 1874 Swiss engineer Nicholas Riggenbach built a standard-gauge railway up the Kahlenberg, near Vienna, with a maximum gradient of 1 in 10 (10 per cent). The rack was laid between the running rails and was constructed in the form of a ladder with wrought iron rungs riveted into the webs of shaped girders placed back to back, about 5in. apart. The rack was constructed of 10ft. lengths, joined by fishplates and bolted to the sleepers. The running rails, of the flat bottomed type, weighing 40lb. per yd., were secured to the sleepers by spikes.

The engine used on this line was built by the Swiss Locomotive Works, Winterthur, and was carried on four wheels, 26in. diameter. The outside horizontal cylinders, 13in. diameter by 17in. stroke, drove a countershaft carrying a pair of pinions. Below the counter-shaft was another shaft carrying three toothed wheels. The central wheel engaged with the rack – the side wheels with the pinions above them. An ordinary locomotive-type boiler was used with a steam pressure of 132lb. per square inch.

The carriages were pushed up the incline by the engine and no couplings were used. Three independent methods of braking were employed. A band brake was used on one of the crank discs. A toothed wheel on the back axle geared with the rack, and the axle was fitted with drums and brake blocks. The third method made use of the compression of air in the engine cylinders. Air was drawn in through the exhaust ports and forced out through a special regulating valve. Another safety precaution was the fitting of guards to prevent derailment.

The ladder type of rack was not without defects, and in 1882 Mr R. Abt patented an improved form of rack in which teeth were cut in the edges of narrow rectangular bars. These bars were placed in pairs, teeth uppermost, on chairs bolted to the sleepers. The teeth of the rack bars were arranged so that they were 'out of step' – the teeth of one rack being adjacent to indents on the other. A pair of stepped pinions on the locomotive engaged with the double rack, and so smoothness of action was ensured. The first line to use the Abt system was built in 1884 at Blankenberg, in the Harz mountains. In 1894-96 a rack railway on this principle was built on Mount Snowdon in Wales.

A typical Swiss-built locomotive for use on an Abt rack railway is carried on six wheels. The four leading wheels run loose on their axles and the trailing wheels are mounted on a Bissell truck. There are two cylinders, placed midway along the engine above the footplating. The drive is of rather unusual design. The piston rods are made very long to reach the cross-heads at the front of the engine. The crossheads actuate cranks on the central axle through connecting rods and rocking levers pivoted low down on the frame.

The two leading axles are coupled by rods and on each is a double pinion, gearing with the rack. It is, of course, the axle pinions that transmit the power – the wheels are for carrying purposes only. The double pinions are interesting, since they are permitted a slight up and down movement, independently of the axles. This is attained by using a pair of toothed rings, placed one either side of a circular disc forged solid with the axle. The movement of the pinions is permitted by use of internal springs. To ensure smooth running the teeth of one pinion are adjacent to the spaces on the other – the usual practice with the Abt system. The pinions are held in place laterally by grooved brake drums, bolted on either side to the axle discs.

The engine resembles the Riggenbach locomotive, since it pushes its train up the mountain side. There are no couplings, and three forms of brake are available. These comprise brake blocks that grip the drums on the driving axles, an automatic brake acting on two of the drums when the speed exceeds 5mph, and the use of compressed air in the cylinders as on the Riggenbach engine. The last-named method is generally used and, since the compression generates heat, the air in the cylinders is cooled by means of water jets.

The boiler of the engine is inclined at an angle of 1 in 11 to obtain a comparatively level surface to the water on steep gradients. The pressure is 200lb. per sq. in. The side water tanks carry 440 gallons, and the coal bunker 10cwt. of fuel. The engine, which weighs in working order 17 tons 4cwt., can propel a load of 18.5 tons at four to five miles an hour.

viii) Rack locomotives do not have to be small! No. 4282 is one of four 0-8-4T, built by the Vienna Locomotive Works, Floridsdorf in 1896 and 1900 for the Hungarian State Railways (MAV). They were at the time the most powerful rack locomotives in Europe. The line they were constructed for ran from Theissholz to Bries, a distance of 41km, with gradients of up to 1 in 20. Due to the sharp curves on the line, the locos had a flexible wheelbase on the Lindner system. Their maximum speed was 25km/hr on level track, and 12km/hr on the rack section. Following border adjustments after World War 1 the line and the locos became the property of Czechoslovakian railways; the last of them was supplanted by diesels in 1964. *(b/w printed card, published Budapest)*

ix) Another giant among mountain railway locos was Prussian State Railways (KPEV) No. 9101. The KPEV operated railways across Germany and into areas now part of Poland and Russia, including several mountainous areas. The locomotive is a standard gauge four-cylinder compound rack-and-adhesion locomotive and was built by Borsig in 1924. It later had its rack gear removed and was sold into private ownership in 1929, surviving to become the property of the East German State Railways (DR) in 1949.

(b/w photographic card, published Berlin)

Another rack system was used on the railway up Mount Pilatus, near Lucerne, Switzerland. The Pilatus line, constructed in 1886-88, was so steep that a double rack - devised by Dr E. Locher was employed. The rack is double, as in the Abt system, but is placed horizontally with the teeth on both sides instead of on top. The Pilatus line is two and three quarters miles long and rises 5,347ft., with a maximum gradient of 1 in 2. To carry passengers up an incline of this nature every possible precaution had to be taken to ensure safety, and the Pilatus steam car incorporates a number of highly ingenious safety devices.

The underframe of the car is carried on four wheels. These are not power driven and are for carrying only. Contrary to expectations, the wheels are flangeless, a feature necessitated by the remarkable sharp curves of the route. The car is prevented from leaving the track by means of the central guide that carries the double-sided rack. The underframe carries at the lower end a pair of horizontal driving wheels on vertical shafts, one on either side of the central rail and rack. Each driving wheel comprises a lower ring that rolls on the side of the central rail and an upper toothed portion gearing with the rack. The rings are of sufficiently large diameter to prevent the wheels from rising out of gear.

Another pair of similar wheels at the front end of the frame is used to guide the car and to work the automatic brake. The pinion wheels at the lower end of the car are driven by two horizontal cylinders through a crankshaft and gearing. The boiler is of the locomotive type, placed across the frame, and works at a pressure of 176lb. per sq. in. The brakes that control a descending car are a hand brake on one of the engine cranks, a cylinder air brake as on the Abt locomotive, and an automatic brake that acts on a drum. The drum is connected with the front pair of toothed wheels by worm gearing. The brake comes into operation automatically should the speed exceed 3mph, and can also be applied by the brakesman on the front of the car. As an additional safeguard the car is fitted with clips embracing the running rails, to guard against derailments by wind. The car weighs 10 tons in working order, and carries 176 gallons of water and 2cwt. of coal. The normal speed of the car is two and a quarter miles an hour.

Another method enabling engines to climb mountainous railways is the "Fell" system, widely used in many parts of the world. This method of increasing the adhesion of locomotives by means of a central rail was proposed by Mr J. B. Fell during the construction of the Mont Cenis Tunnel. Patents for the special locomotives were granted to Mr Fell in 1863-69, and a line was built over the Mont Cenis Pass. The railway was laid along the public road for a distance of 48 miles with a maximum gradient of 1 in 12, and was opened in 1868. The Fell line was not, however, a financial success, and was replaced with a conventional adhesion railway when the Mont Cenis Tunnel was opened in 1871.

The locomotive used on this line was carried on four-coupled wheels, 2ft 4in diameter, driven by a pair of 16in. by 16in. horizontal cylinders. The cylinders were placed inside the frames with the valve chests between them. Valves were driven by outside eccentrics, link motion, and rocking shafts.

The additional adhesion was obtained by means of a central rail laid on all gradients as steep at 1 in 25. The central rail was gripped on either side by a pair of 2ft 4in wheels, pressed inwards by springs and levers, operated by screw gear from the footplate. Each pair of vertical shafts was held in a sliding frame between two transverse stays placed near the middle of the engine. At the upper ends of the shafts were overhung cranks, and the gripping wheels were fixed to the lower ends. The shafts on either side of the central rail were coupled by rods at the top and bottom, and were driven direct from the engine cylinders.

x) X14 is one of five metre gauge 0-8-2T's built by SLM, Winterthur in 1952 for the Nigiri Railway in India, an Abt rack system. They are compound locomotives with all four cylinders outside the frames. The low pressure cylinders, driving the rack wheels, are immediately above the high pressure cylinders. On the easier sections of the line, with no rack rail, the locos work as two cylinder simple engines. *(b/w photographic, SLM "Official")*

xi) This Esslingen 0-4-0T built for the Salzburg-Gaisburg Riggenbach line in Austria displays some interesting detail variations from the Langres locomotive depicted in illus. vi. *(b/w printed card, F Fleury)*

The motion of the crossheads was communicated to the carrying wheels through rocking shafts, levers and outside connecting rods. The boiler pressure was 120lb. per sq. in. and the weight of the engine, in working order, about 20 tons. The pressure of the wheels against the centre rail was also some 20 tons, thus doubling the adhesion. The engine was capable of hauling a load of 20 tons up a gradient of 1 in 12 at a speed of 10 miles an hour. The central rail was double-headed and was laid on its side, supported on chairs of bent wrought iron bars.

Braking was effected by blocks acting on the carrying wheels and also by means of slipper blocks that gripped the centre rail. The Fell system was also used on the famous Rimutaka incline on the North Island of New Zealand.

In another system, invented by the Swiss engineer Wetli, additional rails were laid between the track rails in the form of inverted V's, with the apexes pointing up the incline. A double helix on a drum beneath the engine, driven by the cylinders, engaged with the V's and so propelled the locomotive forward. The helix may be regarded as a raised V round the drum. The Wetli system has not been used in practice chiefly because of the difficulty in laying the V's sufficiently accurately to ensure smooth working. In addition, it was not suitable for use on small-radius curves.

Rack engines have been improved in detail of design since they were first evolved, particularly when electric traction is employed, but the working principles of the various systems have remained unchanged. The rack rail is an ingenious device for overcoming the difficulties encountered by railway engineers in mountainous country, but high speeds are naturally out of the question. Even on the relatively speedy Visp-Zermatt line the rate on the steepest rack section falls to 10mph or less, but the grade of 1 in 8 could not be climbed by a locomotive relying on adhesion alone.

Pre-eminent among manufacturers of rack locomotives was the Swiss firm of SLM, Winterthur. SLM's 1900 Catalogue prominently featured their successful designs. This page depicts a selection of rack-and-adhesion locomotives delivered to customers in Switzerland, Italy, Germany and Hungary.   *(Author's collection)*

Opened in 1896, the 2ft 7^1/$_2$in gauge Snowdon Mountain Railway connected Llanberis with the summit of Snowdon, and was the first (and only) railway in Britain to be equipped with the Abt rack system. **[1]** A real photographic card, produced in 1935 by noted railway photographer R. A. Wheeler, shows No. 7 AYLWIN, one of the second group of locomotives supplied by SLM in 1922-23, easily distinguished from the same builder's earlier design by the much smaller side tanks. The train is awaiting departure from Llanberis on 6th July 1935, a fortunately fine day no doubt welcomed by the passengers, who even at this late date enjoy little weather protection in the open coaches. These were built to a Swiss design intended to provide minimal wind resistance. **[2]** A black and white printed card by the prolific Dundee publisher J. Valentine & Co., depicting a train just beginning the descent from the summit, and graphically illustrating the bleakness of the terrain. On early and late season days, this area is often wreathed in fog, making it impossible to operate trains over the whole line.

By Tram to Snaefell. I.o.M.

3

Having pipped the Snowdon Mountain Railway at the post by opening a year earlier, in 1895, the Snaefell Mountain Railway on the Isle of Man became Britain's first scenic mountain railway. Of 3ft 6in gauge, the railway was 4 miles and 53 chains long, with 85% of its route being at a gradient of 1 in 12, and the remainder varying between 1 in 15 and 1 in $42\frac{1}{2}$. The Fell system was adopted, but the additional power available with electric traction made the additional driving wheels on the Fell rail unnecessary, the cars using normal adhesion power only. The Fell machinery was retained however as a safety braking system. **[3]** This colour tinted card, published in the Baur's series, and posted in 1906, shows one of the Milnes (Birkenhead) cars in original red, white and teak livery and carrying the legend SNOWDON MOUNTAIN TRAMWAY. Unusually in Britain, right hand running is practised, so our car is descending the mountain. **[4]** A sepia card published by the MER itself and probably sold at the Summit Hotel, depicted at an unknown date in the 1950's. The scene is little changed since 1906, though the cars now sport a darker livery.

Station Hotel and Waiting Rooms, Snaefell Mountain Summit, I.O.M.
(2034 feet above sea level)

4

5

[5] The Austrian State Railways' Semmering route was a triumph of engineering achievement in the pioneering days of Europe's railways. Part of a through route from the Austria-Hungarian capital Vienna to Trieste, the line climbs on gradients averaging 1 in 40 for $17^{1}/_{2}$ miles to the summit at Semmering. Electric locomotives now power the trains but this b/w printed card published in Vienna depicts two Kreigslok 2-10-0's at the head of train E983 crossing the Lechnergrabenviaduct in 1953. [6] The 19.5km Erzbergbahn was opened in 1891 by the Lokalbahn Eisenerz-Vordernberg, principally to convey iron ore from the Erzberg (iron mountain) to steelworks at Donawitz. The line had a maximum gradient of 1 in 9 and the Abt rack system was fitted to 14.6km of the route. The line was later absorbed into the ÖBB and offered the visitor the rare treat of being propelled by a steam rack locomotive, on standard gauge, on a normal service train, well into the 1970's. On this photographic card (P. Adlington) 2-6-2T No. 97213 prepares to leave Vordernberg Markt with a passenger train for Eisenerz. The start of the rack system is just visible on the left.

6

The metre gauge Schafbergbahn connects the steamer terminal on Lake Wolfgang with Schafberg summit. 5.8km in length, it opened in 1893 and was originally operated by the Salzkammergut Lokalbahn A.G. Now part of the ÖBB, the line operates an intensive service in summer only, with as many as half a dozen trains travelling in convoy at busy times. **[7]** This black and white printed card published in Salzburg, not postally used but bearing the "Hotel Schafberg Spitze" rubber stamp, gives a good view of the toothed rack rail, with the help of which No. 997306 is propelling its train. The maximum gradient is 1 in 4 (25 per cent), limiting trains to one coach. **[8]** A much photographed view of the summit station, showing the impressive summit hotel complex which dwarfs the modest facilities at Snowdon and Snaefell. This colour printed card, also published in Salzburg, depicts one of the 2099 class rack fitted diesel railcars used to supplement steam workings on the Schafberg, and also on the Puchberg-Hochschneeberg line.

[9] Opened in 1889, the metre gauge Achenseebahn is one of the few railways in this book (the Snaefell being another example) which is still operating, a century after opening, with near original motive power. 6.8km in length, the railway connects Jenbach, on the Innsbruck to Salzburg route, with the inland 'sea' from which it derives its name. Operation is on the Riggenbach system, an operating curiosity is that while trains are propelled in the usual way from Jenbach, on reaching Eben summit the loco runs round and pulls the train on to Achensee. This b/w printed card by Tiroler Kunstverslag, Innnsbuck depicts a downhill train behind loco No. 1 on the Achensee-Eben section, with the lake visible behind. **[10]** The metre gauge Stubitailbahn operates out of its own station in Innsbruck and climbs from 1,932ft to Fulpmes, 11 miles distant at an altitude of 3,014ft, crossing en route a summit af 3,287ft at Telfes. Steepest gradient is 1 in 22 and pure adhesion is used, consequently the railway features numerous hairpin bends and loops and a number of viaducts, favourite subjects for postcard publishers. The Kreist bridge is depicted on this b/w printed card by Fritz Gratl, Innsbruck.

ITALY

[11] Neatly bridging the gap between Austria and Italy is the Rittnerbahn, a metre gauge line opened on 13th August 1907. It ran from Bozen (925m) to Klobenstein (1190m) and comprised 4.1km of rack and 7.64km of adhesion section. The line was electrified at 750 volts from opening. The area was ceded by Austria to Italy after World War 1 and Bozen renamed Bolzano. This attractive colour card published by John F. Amonn, Bozen, depicts the line in Austrian ownership with one of the 4-wheel electric locos running round two of the unusual bogie coaches, which are fully enclosed but feature open balconies. **[12]** In surroundings far more typical of Italy is the Stresa – Lake Maggiore tramway. This was a metre gauge line, electrified at 750v dc, and of its 10km route 3km were adhesion and 7km Strub rack. The line opened in 1911 and closed in 1966. Rolling stock comprised five bogie railcars built by SLM/SIG in 1910/11, one of these is seen hauling a trailer on the rack-fitted stretch of the line, on a b/w photographic card published by Ediz.Orlandini of Stresa.

Napoli · Il Vesuvio-Carozza della Funicolare
Hôtel Weiss
Castellammare. near Naples. *Saturday 9th January*

13

Those who know Thomas Cook Ltd for their timetables and Travel Agencies may be surprised to know that the Company built and operated a railway up the slopes of Italy's Mount Vesuvius. The funicular was a double track monorail, with the running rail riveted on top of timber baulks with iron plated sides. There were two cars ETNA and VESUVIO, each carried by two double flanged wheels astride the track, with two more wheels either side to guide it. The line was 820 metres long with a maximum gradient of 6 per cent. It was replaced by a new funicular in 1903. **[13]** This superb coloured card (E. Ragozino) was posted in January 1909, but presumably printed much earlier. **[14]** A later development was a metre gauge railway, part adhesion, part rack, connecting Pugliaro with the foot of the funicular. The 8km line opened in 1903 and was operated by three 24-seat electric cars, built by Schweitzer Waggon AG of Zurich. The cars had bow collectors and were painted an attractive blue and cream livery. In normal service, an electric locomotive was coupled behind the car to propel it up the 1 in 4 gradient of the rack and pinion section. The railway was equipped with larger cars in the 1920's, and operated until 1952, when an improved road brought about its closure.

14

15

The Gotthard Railway was the first route to tackle the mighty barrier posed by the Swiss Alps. The St Gotthard Pass was often blocked in winter, and to take the railway through it would have been impossible. It was decided therefore to drive $9^1/_4$ miles of the route in tunnel under the Alps, a feat never before attempted anywhere else in the world. Construction commenced in 1872 and finished in 1882, with up to 3,400 men at a time working on the tunnel. **[15]** From just over 1,400ft at Lucerne the railway climbs to an altitude of 3,786ft – 200ft higher than Snowdon – in the 18 miles between Erstfeld and summit (which is inside the tunnel). In pre-electrification days loads were understandably light, this full colour card (E. Goetz, Luzern, No 1742) depicts a typical train of the 1900-1910 period behind 4-6-0 No. 202. **[16]** 55 miles from Lucerne is Goschenen and the northern entrance to the tunnel. This b/w card by Photoglob-Wehrli AG, Zurich (No. 5025) depicts a northbound train hauled by electric loco No. 12.311. The line to the right is the Schöllen rack line of the metre gauge Furka-Oberalp Railway.

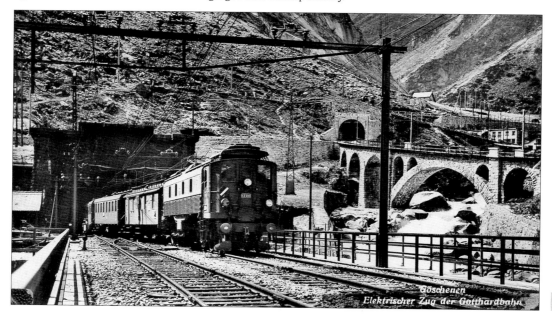

Göschenen
Elektrischer Zug der Gotthardbahn

16

4387. Ferrovia del S. Gottardo.
Galleria spirale del Prato.

17

[17] The statistics of the Gotthard route are awe-inspiring. In its 140 mile route between Lucerne and Chiasso there are (in addition to the Gotthard tunnel itself) a further $9^{1}/_{4}$ miles of tunnels, 79 in all, seven of which incorporate spirals, plus 334 bridges and viaducts. This Photoglöb, Zurich coloured card depicts the section of line south of the Gotthard Tunnel, where the railway falls on a ruling gradient of 1 in 40. To lose height quickly, the railway passes in quick succession through two spiral tunnels, Freggio, and then Prato (1,560m). Close examination of this card shows the entrance to the tunnel at the higher level.

[18] (Opposite page, top) Electrification of the main mountain section had been planned before World War 1 and the first electric hauled trains ran between Erstfeld and Airolo (the southern end of the Tunnel) on 18 September 1920. The whole line was electrified on 29 May 1921. Current was supplied on the single-phase AC system at 15,000 volts. The electric locomotives enabled much heavier trains to be hauled, as well as greatly improving conditions for crew and passengers! This b/w card published by A. & W. Borelli, Airolo depicts Airolo station with the Alps in the background. Incidentally although signs here are in Italian, we are still in Switzerland – the border at Chiasso is over 50 miles to the south.

[19] In 1898 work began on an even more ambitious project, driving a railway beneath the Simplon Pass. This involved a tunnel 12 miles 668 yards in length, then the world's longest. Work began on 1 August on the Swiss side at Brig, and on 16 August on the Italian side at Iselle de Trasquera. The original tunnel was single track, with a parallel auxiliary service tunnel 2.5m in diameter, to help access and improve ventilation – temperatures inside the mountain could reach 129F (50°C). The two workings met on 24 February 1905 and the official opening took place on 17 May 1906. Electric working throughout the tunnel commenced on 1 July 1906, using 3,000 volts AC three-phase. In 1930 the three-phase system was abandoned in favour of the standard SBB single-phase system on 15,000 volts. Despite its scenic attractions the Simplon has attracted far less attention from postcard publishers. This attractive colour card by Phototypie 158, posted in Zermatt in 1911, shows a southbound train emerging from the tunnel behind an early three-phase electric loco. Hidden behind the train, the former service tunnel on the left is being enlarged to form a second tunnel; work on this was held up by the First World War and eventual opening to traffic was in December 1921.

158   Brigue. Entrée du tunnel du Simplon

Rigi-Staffel (1600 m) und Kulm (1800) m
mit Vierwaldstätter- u. Zugersee

In 1863 Swiss engineer Nicholas Riggenbach took out a patent involving the installation of a steel ladder, or rack, between the running lines. The locomotive, instead of using conventional driving wheels, would be equipped with vertical toothed wheels, or pinions, driven by steam cylinders and engaging the rack, thus the title 'rack and pinion'. Riggenbach was however beaten at the post by Sylvester Marsh (see p. 59), whose railway equipped with a similar system had opened at Mount Washington in 1867. Losing no more time, Riggenbach obtained the concession to build a rack and pinion railway from Vitznau, on the north shore of Lake Lucerne, up the west side of the Rigi, with a gradient of 1 in 5, to Kaltbad, at the north-west corner of the Rigi range, there turning north-east to Staffel and Rigi-Kulm. The line opened in 1871. **[20]** At Staffel the Rigi-bahn was joined by a competing line, the Arth-Rigi Railway, the two lines meeting on the far side of the hotel depicted on this b/w card published by Photoglob-Wehrli and showing the line in later days after electrification. **[21]** Both railways built their own lines the final mile to the summit, this coloured card published by E. Goetz, Luzern, posted in 1913 shows the 'double track' section.

Die Rigibahn und die Berneralpen.

12044. Elektr. Bahn Stansstad-Engelberg.

[22] About 22 miles south of Lucerne lies the mountain resort of Engelberg. Access to the outside world was by the metre gauge Stansstad-Engelberg railway, a rack and adhesion line starting at Stansstad (reached originally from Lucerne by Lake steamers) and serving en route the state capital Stans. Electrified at 850 volts dc, the line included a one mile stretch where the railway was lifted 958ft into the Engelberg valley basin by a rack and pinion section at 1 in 4, from Obermatt up to Gherst. As the motor coaches had no rack equipment, it was necessary to attach a rack fitted 'banker' to propel the cars up this section! In the 1960's the railway was extended back to a junction with the metre gauge SBB Brünig line at Hergiswil, involving the boring of a tunnel 1,925 yards in length, and considerable major engineering works on the rest of the line. The railway was also re-electrified at 15,000 volts dc and completely re-equipped with new trains that can perform the Lucerne-Engelberg run in as little as 55 mins. Our coloured card published by Verlag Wehrli-AG, Zurich (No. 10244) is a reminder of a less hurried era when the journey by steamer and railway took around two hours.

23 Wengernalpbahn mit Jungfrau.

South of Interlaken lies a group of justly-famed mountain railways. Commencing at Lauterbrunnen (junction with the metre gauge Bernese-Oberland Bahn line from Interlaken) the 80cm (2ft 7^1/$_2$ in) gauge Wengeralpbahn climbs on a ruling gradient of 1 in 5 (20 per cent) through Wengen and Wengernalp to Kleine Schiedegg, a distance of 6^1/$_2$ miles, during which the train has ascended 4,147ft. Here it makes an end-on connection with the Railway's other arm, which starts from Grindelwald and climbs 3,665ft in 4^1/$_2$ miles, using rack and pinion propulsion throughout. Here the maximum gradient is 1 in 4 (25 per cent). **[23]** A superb view on a colour card (R Garbler, Interlaken) bearing a Wengernalp-Schiedegg postmark and posted on 27 July 1906, shows one of the line's original rack-fitted tanks propelling a train up from Lauterbrunnen, with the 13,600ft high Jungfrau mountain dominating the view ahead. **[24]** An equally attractive view, taken after electrification and published in colour by the prolific Wehrli-AG, Zurich, shows one of the early electric locos pausing at Wengernalp station.

24684 Wengernalp m. Eiger u. Mönch.

24

Kleine Scheidegg (2064 m) mit Wetterhorn (3703 m)

[25] Kleine Schiedegg, seen here on a b/w card by Wehrli, is a narrow gauge 'Clapham Junction' where Wengernalp trains make connection with the Jungfrau line. Perhaps the most famous mountain railway in the world, the metre gauge Jungfraubahn was the vision of a Zurich businessman, Herr Guyer-Zeller, who observed the success of the Wengern line and concluded there would be even greater demand for a line to the Jungfrau summit. The project was dismissed as impossible and was only accomplished by utilising a winding route, numerous tunnels, and locating the summit station, Jungfraujoch (11,333ft) inside the mountain itself. The final tunnel, hacked through solid rock and ice, took six years to complete. **[26]** This colour card (Photoglob, Zurich) provides an excellent view of Eigertletscher station, 954ft above Kleine Scheidegg, reached by a journey on a continuous gradient of 1 in 4. Ascending trains continue through a short tunnel to Eigerwand, where a stop is made to allow passengers to look down on Grindelwald 6,000ft below. There is a further stop at Eisneer before the train enters the subterranean terminus. The line is rack and pinion thoughout and has been electrified from opening at 5,000 volts dc.

Schynige Platte-Bahn.
Aussicht auf Breitlauenen, Niesen und Thunersee
8383 Phototypie Co., Neuchâtel

[27] Two miles from Interlaken on the Bernese-Oberland-Bahn is the station of Wilderswil. This is the starting point of the Schynige Platte Railway, a rack and pinion line which ascends 4,537ft in $4^1/_2$ miles, on a ruling gradient of 1 in 4 (25 per cent). The railway threads a heavily forested route with excellent views over the Thunersee, and from the summit can be seen the Schreckhorn, Eiger, Mönch and Jungfrau mountains. Our coloured card (Phototypie Co., Neuchâtel, No. 8383) shows one of the early steam locos, supplanted in the 1930's by electric traction. The coach running board was used by the conductor to check tickets en route, even when the train ran alongside a precipice!

[28] At Lauterbrunnen the traveller can join a cable hauled funicular, at the summit of which will be found the totally isolated Mürrenbahn. This runs for $3^1/_2$ miles, high above the cliffs on the west side of the Lauterbrunnen valley, to the resort of Mürren. This early card (R. Gabler, Interlaken, No. 1091) gives a good view of the 4-wheel OHW loco and the rather unusual coach, its centre portion completely open at the sides. Provisions, including beer barrels, are carried on the rear balcony.

Pilatusbahn. Wolfort-Viadukt

[29] Fired by Riggenbach's success on the Rigi (see p 26), another engineer, Locher, decided to tackle the even more difficult task of building a railway to the summit of Pilatus. This line climbs 5,355ft in only 2.6 miles, requiring an average gradient of about 1 in $2^1/_2$, and a steepest grade of 48% – almost 1 in 2. At such an inclination even the Riggenbach rack would not have been safe, Locher's system (described in CONQUEST OF THE CLOUDS) used horizontal pinions on the locomotive to grip the rack from both sides. Due to the steep gradient the locomotive's boiler could not be set lengthwise in the usual fashion and was placed crosswise, with its water supply carried in a compartment built into the coach underframe. These novel features are shown to good effect in this coloured card (E. Goetz, Luzern), posted in July 1937 and with a message describing the trip on the railway as "a thrilling affair."

[30] Rounding off our collection of rack and pinion railways is the Brienz Rothorn Bahn, connecting Brienz with Rothorn summit, 7,349ft. Unlike the other Swiss railways featured, the BRB has remained predominantly steam operated to the present day. This coloured card by Photoglob-Wehrli shows SLM No. 6 on the final few yards of the climb into the summit station.

On the eastern side of Switzerland can be found the Rhaetian Railway (Rhätischebahn). Opened in stages between 1890 and 1913, the railway consists of some 244 route miles and boasts 108 tunnels, plus numerous loops and spirals. Many of the towns served are ski resorts and the railway takes pride in year-round operation, despite the prevalent snow. Jewel in the RhB's crown is the Bernina line, the highest through route in Europe. The 61km line was opened in 1910 and connects St. Moritz with Tirano, Italy, crossing en route a summit at 7,408ft at Bernina Hospice. Ruling gradient is 1 in 14 and operation is entirely by adhesion, the route having been electrified from opening. **[31]** This attractive 'official' card bearing the Bahnhofbuffet Berninahospiz franking, depicts a train arriving at the summit station in 1934. **[32]** The RhB's other routes were steam worked initially. This Locomotive Publishing Co. sepia card was published in the 'Locomotive Magazine' series and depicts 2-4-4-0 Mallet locomotive No. 26, one of eight built by SLM in 1902 in preparation for the opening of the lines to Ilanz and St.Moritz. Displaced by electrification in 1920, No. 26 was sold to the Yverdon-Ste Croix Railway and sold on in 1947 to the Puertollano-Penarroya Railway in Spain, finally being scrapped in 1954.

33

[33] A close neighbour of the RhB is the metre gauge Furka-Oberalp Railway. Construction of the line started in 1911 and was not completed until 1925. The single track line has 11 separate rack sections totalling 32km, and the maximum gradient is 1 in 9. In its 100km route from Brig to Disentis the railway utilises 15 tunnels, 77 viaducts and bridges, and numerous loops and spirals. This modern coloured card shows one of the more pastoral sections of the route at Hospental, and a typical train of lightweight stock hauled by a series HGe4/4 series 31 Bo-Bo, of the type that has handled all traffic since 1942. [34] Sole metre gauge route of the Swiss Federal Railways is the Brünig line, from Lucerne to Interlaken Ost, serving en route Sarnes, Brienz and Meringen. The line was constructed in stages from 1885 to 1916. In its 74km route the railway threads 13 tunnels and crosses 22 major bridges and viaducts. Most of its route is adhesion worked, but there are several sections of Riggenbach rack, with a maximum gradient of 1 in 9. The summit is at Brünig-Hasliberg, 3,287ft. The railway was electrified in 1941-2, this photographic card by H. W. Wheeler dated 10 August 1937 depicting 0-6-2 rack tank No. 215 at Interlaken Ost has captured the final years of the steam era.

34

TROUBLE WITH SNOW

[35] A glorious sepia card, posted in 1939, showing a rotary snowplough of the Berninabahn, Switzerland, in action. Note the wall of cleared snow (right). *(sepia, real photo, Engaden Press, St Moritz)*

[36] Similar conditions being tackled on the Denver and Rio Grande 3ft gauge Silverton line in Colorado, USA, using a 'wedge' plough. *(b/w, real photo, Rocky Mountain View Co., Denver)*

37

[37] Manual methods are evidently contemplated to rescue this train on the Rigibahn, Switzerland. *(sepia printed card, unknown publisher)*

38

[38] A rotary snowplough at Rousses, on the now closed French section of the Nyon-Morez line in 1950. *(b/w printed card, BVA Lausanne)*

39 J. J. 8590 Chamonix — Chemin de fer du Montenvers et le Mont-Blanc

18km from the Swiss border, on the metre gauge Col des Montets line from St Gervais le Fayet to Vallorcine, lies the health resort of Chamonix. This is the starting point of the CF Chamonix-Montenvers, a 3^1/$_4$ mile metre gauge line opened throughout on 29 May 1909, and electrified in 1954, on 11,000volts AC. The strub rack system is used and the maximum gradient is 1 in 4.5 (22 per cent). The railway's raison d'être is to carry tourists up the 871 metre ascent to the 'Mer de Glace' (sea of ice) where three major glaciers meet. **[39]** Original motive power comprised eight identical 2-4-0T's built by SLM (Winterthur), weighing 22 tonnes and developing 250hp, enabling the locos to propel a two-coach train when necessary. This sepia card (Jullien frères, Geneva) shows an ascending train behind No. 4, and gives a good view of the strub rack. An unexplained curiosity, not present on other cards, is the roofboard on the coach roof. **[40]** At the palatial terminal station, passengers change to a cable car to descend to the 'Mer de Glace'. This b/w printed card is produced by the topographical publisher Lucien Levy (LL), whose prolific coverage of French towns includes a number of excellent railway views.

40 27 CHAMONIX-MONT-BLANC. - Mer de Glace. - LL

[41] From St Gervais les Bains the metre gauge Tramway de Mont Blanc begins its 12.4km ascent to the slopes of Mont Blanc. Using the strub rack system, the TMB was opened in 1914. The line was electrified in 1957, on 11,000volts AC, 50HZ. Three motor cars were ordered from SLM (Winterthur) and paired with trailers built by Decauville. In best 'narrow gauge' tradition these are different in outline, giving the trains a pleasing 'second-hand' appearance. The TMB has boasted a succession of rather gaudy liveries, this full colour card published in Paris shows a two-tone blue and orange livery. The train is on the Bellevue plateau, close to the upper terminus. [42] Along the French side of the Pyrenees there are, or have been, a number of mountain railways and funiculars. One that has survived, virtually unchanged, is the rack line from St Ignace (279m) to La Rhune (910m), route length $4^{1}/_{2}$ km. Work on the line started in 1912 and, delayed somewhat by World War 1, opening was on 20 June 1924. Stock consists of 6 motor coaches and 6 trailers, and it is believed this is the original equipment. This modern coloured card shows an ascending train with a panorama of St Jean-de-Luz and the Atlantic coast beyond.

AIX-LES-BAINS. - La Gare du Revard - LL

[43] The metre gauge rack railway from Aix-les-Bains (in the south of France between Annecy and Chambéry) to Le Mont Revard opened on 15 August 1892. It was 9.1km in length and used the Abt rack system. Le Revard terminus was at an altitude of 1511m. The line was an early casualty of bus competition, closing in May 1936. Lucien Levy published several cards of the line, this one shows the terminus at Aix-les-Bains. [44] One of the most obscure railways to feature in this book must be the CF à Crémaillère de la Turbie. The metre gauge Riggenbach rack line connected Beausoleil, somewhat inland of Monte Carlo centre, and just outside of the Principality, with La Turbie, 2.6km away at a height of 500m. The railway closed on 8 March 1932 following a fatal accident, but the stock and track remained in situ for many years afterwards. There is a wealth of detail interest in this superb card by Aqua Photo, Paris: the staggered buffer beam with its large headlight; the footboard and steps on the coach sides; and (just visible) the cog wheel under the coach engaging the rack ladder.

3291 Côte d'Azur. La Turbie. Chemin de fer à crémaillère.

60 LANGRES. — *Chemin de fer à crémaillère sur le Pont.* — *Railway on the bridge* — LL

[45] The CF à Crémaillère de Langres connected Langres (Marne) station with the old walled city above. It was one of the earliest lines to be built on the Riggenbach system, Riggenbach himself designing the original stock, and supervising the line's construction. Built in 1887, it was partly adhesion worked, with sections of rack, as seen here on a LL card depicting the line's major engineering feature, a handsome concrete viaduct. **[46]** The metre gauge system on the island of Corsica totals some 350km and consists of a lengthy route connecting the two main towns, Bastia and Ajaccio, together with a secondary line to Calvi. Bastia and Ajaccio are both at sea level and the line connecting them features a constant succession of sharp curves, loops, bridges and viaducts, one tunnel 2 miles 762 yards long and gradients up to 1 in 30. Vecchio, 56 miles from Bastia, is at a height of 1558ft. Vecchio viaduct, illustrated on a sepia card by Cartes la Cigorne, Ajaccio, is 459ft long and 262ft above the river. From here there is a continuous climb for 7 miles at 1 in 33 to Vivario. Further on the gradient steepens to 1 in 30 and the summit level is reached at Vizzavona, 2,972ft.

[47] The fortified city of Laon stands at some height above its SNCF station and, as at Langres, there was a demand for transportation from station to town. The metre gauge CF de Laon was built in 1899 and was adhesion worked, but with an Abt rack for braking purposes only on part of the route. It was electrified from the outset, this b/w card (Cie des Arts Photomécaniques, Paris) shows one of the cars near the summit, with the rack clearly visible. [48] The Nyon-St Cergue-Morez Railway linked Nyon in S.W. Switzerland with the frontier town of La Cure and continued to Morez in France, crossing en route the 1233m high Givrine Pass. The line is metre gauge, adhesion worked, with a maximum gradient of 1 in 16 (6 per cent). Opened in stages between 1916 and 1921, the railway was electrically worked from the outset at 2200 volts dc, motive power being ADBe 4/4 Bo-Bo motor cars built by Schweitzerische Wagenfabrik Schlieren in 1914. This unusual b/w card (a 'modern' reproduction of a period photo) records an incident in 1943 when the track was sabotaged by the French resistance, resulting in the derailment of car No. 5 at La Doye. Damage appears modest, but falling traffic ultimately led to closure of the French section in the 1960's.

17 LA SCHLUCHT [alt. 1159 m] - La Gare du Tramway électrique et l'Hôtel

[49] Situated to the south of Nancy, not far from the Swiss border, this is one of the lesser known mountain railways of France. Of metre gauge, it extended from Gérardmer (alt. 671m) to La Schlucht (1150m), with a reversal to reach Le Hohneck (1366m). The line was electrified at 550volt dc and the mountain section from Retornemer required powerful bogie cars equipped with electro-magnetic brakes. This section was electrified when constructed about 1905, but the 'valley' section was steam operated until 1928. The line only operated in summer, the climatic conditions in winter making for adhesion problems. Sadly, the line was badly damaged during World War 2 and never reopened. This beautiful printed card by Boehler, La Schlucht shows a two car train made up of highly distinctive stock. **[50]** Also metre gauge, the Cie de Tramways de Bigorre operated two lines from Bagneres-de-Bigorre to Lourdes and Artigues, in the Hautes Pyrenees region. The original concession dates from 1903 and the system closed in 1932, having never been profitable; this view of the terminus at Artiges – the only two-story building on the system – sums up the bleakness of the terrain served. The car is believed to be a bogie motor coach of the Al-4 series, as operating before 1924 when a disastrous fire at Bagneres depot brought about the rebuilding of much of the stock. This b/w card is locally produced, though the name is indistinct.

LES HAUTES-PYRÉNÉES

1626. - BAGNÈRES-DE-BIGORRE - GRIPP

LA GARE DU TRAMWAY DE BAGNÈRES A GRIPP – VUE VERS BAGNÈRES

A Selection of Funiculars

[51] The vertiginous ascent at Terriet-Glion, Switzerland was not for the faint-hearted! *(b/w printed card, Charnaux-Frères & Co, Geneva)*

[52] A more gently graded line serving the pic du Ger above Lourdes, France. *(coloured card, Levy Fils & Cie., Paris, s/w 232)*

[53] Tibidabo in Barcelona, which connects a tramway route with the large amusement park at the summit. *(b/w printed card, L. Roisin, Barcelona)*

[54] Also connecting with a municipal tram service is the H&B Incline Railway in Hamilton, Ontario, Canada. *(printed sepia card, International Stationery Co., Picton)*

55

[55] Spain is a land of diversity and a haven of the unpredictable, not least in the field of narrow gauge railways. Some 20 miles inland from the Costa Brava at Barcelona, a rack railway linked Monistrol, on the Catalanes metre gauge system, with the ancient town of Montserrat. Primarily to cater for the large number of pilgrims and tourists visiting the Monastery (situated at 3,725ft asl), a 8km. metre gauge rack railway was built between 1892 and 1905, using the Abt rack system. Motive power consisted of Cail and SLM 0-4-2T's, one of the latter being obtained from the Gornergrat Railway in Switzerland. Sadly, in contrast with the flourishing trade on the Swiss mountain lines, traffic on the Montserrat railway dwindled to the stage where it was declared uneconomical and closed down in 1957. Numerous postcard publishers were attracted to the line by the dog 'Bobi' which was trained by its crossing keeper owner to pose in a begging position (complete with railway 'uniform') at an intermediate station. Of rather more interest to the enthusiast is this lovely colour view of the summit station, with 2 or possibly 3 trains present. This postcard, unfortunately anonymous, is a design curiousity insofar as its back is taken up entirely with lines for name and address, with no space left for a message.

[56] The 3ft gauge Ferrocarril de Soller connects Palma, the capital of Majorca, with the north coast resort of Soller. Opened in 1911, the railway was steam worked, but electric traction took over in 1929, and the railway continues to operate, with its original equipment, virtually unchanged today. The most spectacular section of line is after the 1³/₄mile summit tunnel where the railway descends in a series of loops on the last 3 miles into Soller. This coloured card (Iscaria, Palma) shows one of the Carde y Escoriaza motor cars and well filled train climbing out of Palma. [57] The Portuguese island of Madeira is situated in the Atlantic Ocean, some 400 miles off the African mainland. A prime tourist attraction was the 'Monte' (Mount Church) above Funchal, and in 1891-4 a metre gauge railway using the Riggenbach rack system was built to carry tourists 2¹/₂ km from Funchal to Monte (Atalhino). Locomotives by Esslingen and SLM were employed. Unfortunately traffic was badly hit by the opening of a new road in the 1930's and the railway closed in 1939. This anonymous b/w card shows an Esslingen loco at the upper terminus with (right) a 'tea tray,' a type of sledge controlled by two stalwart men that enabled adventurous passengers to descend to Funchal in 10 minutes – half the time taken by the train!

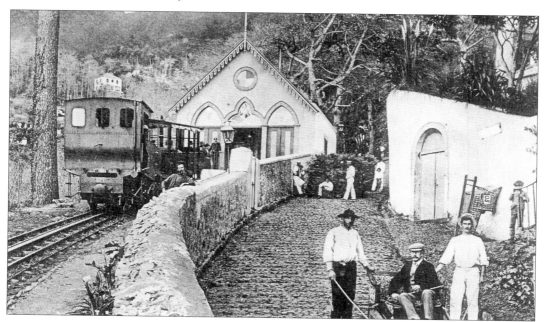

[58] South of Bonn, in the district known as Siebengebirge (Seven Mountains) lies the Drachenfels (Dragon's Rock), 1,065ft high. A metre gauge rack railway to transport visitors was built in the short space of $8^1/_2$ months, between November 1882 and July 1883. The line, commencing at Konigswinter, utilises the Riggenbach rack system, and climbs 220 metres in a total length of 1,520 metres, at an average gradient of 1 in 6.87 (14 per cent). Locomotives were built by Esslingen and incorporated three separate braking systems. Most accounts of the railway mention two coach trains, this photographic card (Hans Andres, Hamburg) is unusual in depicting a three coach train. [59] Operating entirely on adhesion, but demonstrating many of the characteristics of the mountain railway, are the metre gauge Harzquerbahn and Brockenbahn in the Harz mountain area of south-eastern Germany. The main line connects Harzgerode with Wernigerode and a steeply graded line runs from Drei Annen Hohne to Brocken summit. This attractive coloured card by Louis Glasser, Leipzig, posted in Wernigerode on 6 August 1935 shows one of the line's original small Mallets, now supplanted by more modern and powerful steam locomotives.

Harzquerbahn.

59

[60] Jugoslavia, once part of the Austro-Hungarian Empire, had a thriving network of 76cm. gauge railways. Best known of these was the 160 mile long line connecting Dubrovnik with the Bosnian capital, Sarajevo. This was mainly adhesion worked but included a rack section on the northern part near Konjik. Construction of an alternative standard gauge route brought about closure in 1971. This superb photographic card by Alfred Luft perfectly captures the atmosphere of the railway, whose heavy trains – sometimes including dining cars! – often required double heading. The locomotives are two-cylinder compound 83-138 and Austrian built 2-8-2 73-018; the location is Jablanica, and the date is 1959. **[61]** The Zahnradbahn beim Csorber-See opened on 31 July 1896. Situated in the High Tatra area of what is now Slovakia, the railway was of metre gauge and used the Riggenbach rack system. Its two Floridsdorf 0-4-0T locomotives were very similar to those used on Austria's Achenseebahn. This locally produced coloured card, with bilingual caption, (as the area was still then part of the Austro-Hungarian Empire) was posted in 1909. The line closed in 1932 but in 1970 was rebuilt as an electric light railway using Swiss equipment.

GREECE

62

The railways in the Peloponese are of metre gauge but a 750mm gauge part rack line links Diakofto with Kalavrita, a highly scenic ride of some 13¹/₂ miles up the gorge of the Bouraikos. The first 8km are adhesion worked although grades of 1 in 28 are encountered, while on the Abt rack section there are grades of 1 in 7. The railway was built in 1890/91 but not opened until 1896. The first locomotives were 0-6-2 rack engines from Cail, three in 1890 and one in 1900, augmented by one from Krupp in 1925. **[62]** In 1958 three railcar sets arrived from Billard, highly unusual as they consisted of an electric driving car and a trailer, between which was sandwiched a small two axle trailer carrying a diesel generator to supply power to the electric motors. A further trio arrived from Decauville in 1967 and these are still in use today. This locally published photographic card depicts one of the Billard sets. **[63]** A b/w printed card depicting locomotive No. 1. This is an example of a mammoth series – thought to total at least 1324 railway images – produced by the Paris publisher F. Fleury, prior to World War 1. The majority are of French main line railways, but 36 are known to exist of *"Locomotives Diverses,"* (these include minor and industrial railways) and 318 in the series *"Locomotives étrangères"* (railways outside France).

63

LEBANON

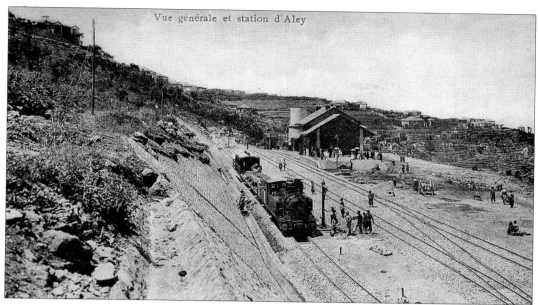

Vue générale et station d'Aley

Railway construction came late to the area now known as the Lebanon, at the time part of the Turkish Ottoman Empire. Prime objective was to link the major port of Beirut with the Syrian capital, Damascus. The line was to the unusual gauge of 1.05m, to match that of the Hedjaz Railway which ran south from Damascus into Jordan. The French construction company bravely opted for the most direct route across the Lebanon mountains, beginning work in 1892, and the line opened throughout in August 1895. From sea level at Beirut the line climbs to a summit of 5,059ft at 38km, then descends to 3,100ft at Rayak, before climbing again to 4,636ft to cross the Anti-Lebanon range. There are several sections of Abt rack between km6 and km47. **[64]** Commercial postcards of the line are extremely rare, this printed card by Dimitri Tarazi & Fils, Beyrouth depicts Aley, one of two reversing stations, and may have been taken in construction days, as some of the works seem unfinished, and the wagon conveys rails. The line remained open as far as Rayak until the 1970's, when the Civil War resulted in its closure. **[65]** The first locomotive was ordered from SLM, Winterthur in 1893 and was a four-cylinder rack-fitted 0-6-2T. It is illustrated here on a F. Fleury card.

189 — Les Locomotives (Turquie d'Asie)
Chemin de Fer du Libanon (Voie de 1 m. 050)

Locomotive à 4 cylindres, à adhérence et à crémaillère (système Abt)
à 6 roues accouplées, essieu porteur arrière
Construite par la Société Suisse pour la construction de Locomotives et Machines Winterthur

AFRICA

66

Our next two illustrations depict narrow gauge railways on the Red Sea coast. **[66]** Massaua, in what was then the Italian colony of Eritrea, is the starting point of the 76cm gauge line to Asmara, the capital. Construction began in 1887, in surroundings among the most hostile to life anywhere on the planet, and finally reached Asmara, 7,143ft asl. and 73 miles away, in 1911. En route are gradients as steep as 1.7 per cent and numerous tunnels and hairpin bends, limiting the original 0-4-4-0 locomotives to haulage of 55 tons. Commercial cards of this line too are scarce, this b/w printed card by M. Fioretti, Asmara shows Massaua in very early days, as evidenced by the full rigged sailing ship. **[67]** Further south lies the port of Djibouti from where a metre gauge line ran to Addis Ababa, capital of Ethiopia. From sea level at Djibouti the line rises 3,920ft at Dire Dawa, then descends to 2,778ft at Awash before climbing again to 7,704ft at Addis. Construction began in 1899 but the difficult terrain, and the onset of World War 1, delayed completion until 1917. Among the first locos were four SLM 2-6-0's, these were outclassed on the mountain section and soon relegated to short distance workings. No. 2 is seen at Addis on a sepia postcard by Fotocelere, Torino, which may date from the short period when the country was under Italian occupation.

67

Summit – Highest point on British Colonial Railways   C. 11

The former British colonies of Kenya, Tanganyika and Uganda were linked together with a fine system of metre gauge railways that connected the Indian Ocean with the hinterland and provided vital communications in the country areas. Most important line was that from of Mombasa to the Kenyan capital, Nairobi, and on to Uganda. From Mombasa the line climbs on a ruling gradient of 2 per cent, with stretches of 1.5 per cent, to reach Nairobi, then ascends rapidly to reach the edge of the Rift Valley. From a summit at 8,000ft the line falls to the valley floor, then after Nakuru climbs again to Mau summit at 9,136ft asl. Such extreme gradients needed powerful locomotives, and were a significant factor in the development of the Beyer-Garratt articulated type. **[68]** This official card, one of a colour series published by East African Railways and Harbours, depicts a small Garratt passing Mau summit. **[69]** An unusual card published by the Farmers' Journal, Nairobi, entitled "a narrow squeak on the Mau" depicts an obviously posed view of an inspection trolley being manhandled from out of the path of an approaching train, rounding a typical curve on the escarpment.

[70]

[70] In present-day Pakistan, then the North Western Frontier Province of India, this sepia photographic card by K. C. Mehra & Sons, Peshawar depicts a HG class 2-8-0 emerging from a tunnel on the famed Khyber Pass railway. This broad gauge line, completed in 1925, fulfilled a vital strategic role by helping to pacify the lawless frontier area. Leaving the Plain of Peshawar at Jamrud, the line climbs 2,000ft to the summit at Landi Kotal, the steepest part of the climb requiring 1 in 33 grades and two reversals. **[71]** Two of the broad gauge lines radiating out from Bombay had to negotiate the Western Ghats, the steep and rugged escarpment on the western side of the Central Indian plateau. The Bhore Ghat incline, on the route from Bombay to Poona, was 16 miles in length, and took the line up 1,800ft. Trains had to surmount 11 miles of 1 in 40, two miles of 1 in 38, and a final two miles of 1 in 40. En route were 25 tunnels totalling 2 miles, eight large viaducts, and a reversing station at Khandala, a popular subject for postcards and shown here on an anonymous b/w card. A later realignment bypassed the reversing station, and the route is now electrified.

[71]

Nilgiri Railway passing near Kullar.

72

Many of India's narrow gauge mountain lines were constructed to serve hill stations, colonised by British civilian and Army personnel during the summer to escape the heat of the plains. In the far south, the metre gauge Nilgiri Railway connects Mettupaliyam with Ootacamund, one-time HQ of the Government of Madras. Promoted by a private company, it opened to Coonoor (16.8 miles) in 1899 and to 'Ooty' (28.7 miles) in 1908. The Swiss Abt rack system was used as far as Coonoor, beyond here the line was adhesion only. An unusual feature is that the locomotive continues to propel the train,even on the non-rack section. **[72]** This b/w printed card, carrying no publisher imprint but printed in Saxony, shows TIGER, one of the early North British rack tanks, and three palatial first class carriages. The train is posed at Kallar, 4.6 miles from Mettupaliyam, and the start of the rack section. **[73]** On the opening of the line, some 0-4-4-0 Mallet locomotives were used, though these had a short life. In the early days of the line trains on the upper section were hauled (not propelled) and this anonymous coloured card shows a train of much more 'basic' stock, including what appears to be a converted bogie wagon.

NEAR RAILWAY STATION OOTACAMUND.

73

74

The small town of Simla, 6870ft asl,was used as summer HQ of both the Supreme Government of India (normally based in Delhi) and the Government of the Punjab. Good communications were vital, and the 2ft 6in gauge railway from Kalka was opened on 9th November 1903. In its 60 mile route the railway includes 103 tunnels totalling 5 miles in length, 869 bridges, numerous reverse curves and gradients up to 1 in 30. The early days of the railway are well illustrated on a series of good quality colour cards published by Moorli Dhur & Sons, Ambala. **[74]** To keep construction costs down, stone was used to construct most of the bridges and viaducts, some of the larger viaducts were built using tiers of arches one above the other. The highest ran to four tiers and is pictured here on card No. 1361. The locomotive is a 2-6-2T which, in several variants, constituted the mainstay of the line's motive power in steam days. **[75]** Barogh station lies at 5020ft and at 26.1 miles was at the end of the first long climb from Kalka Jcn. It was therefore a convenient point for locomotive and passengers to seek respite, and card No. 1369 shows the extensive refreshment facilities provided.

PRINCIPAL STATION BAROOH, HALT FOR REFRESHMENTS

75

76

Perhaps the most famous mountain railway in the world is the Darjeeling-Himalaya. Construction of the 2ft gauge line began in 1879 and proceeded with commendable rapidity, services commencing on 4th July 1881. The railway ascends from 400ft at Siliguri to a summit at Ghoom (7,804ft) before descending into Darjeeling itself. In its 50 mile route are numerous loops and five reversals (zig zags), these combine to make the journey time some 8 hours. **[76]** This interesting b/w printed card, from an anonymous publisher, depicts a very early scene on the line at Mahanadee. On the right is a mixed train hauled by a B class 0-4-0T, with what appears to be an inspection car on the left. The lightweight trackwork, with sleepers already buried up to rail level, will be noted. **[77]** Most publishers concentrated on the 'mountain' section of the line, so it is pleasant to find this b/w photographic card (also anonymous) showing Darjeeling station. This as can be seen was fully enclosed at this time, the overall roof has since disappeared,making this early view particularly valuable.

Railway Station, Darjeeling.

77

THE GOKTEIK GORGE & RAILWAY BRIDGE.

78

[78] Starting from Myohaung Jcn near Mandalay, the Lashio branch of the metre gauge Burma Railways is around 170 miles in length. At Sedaw (15 miles) the climb begins, with four successive reversing stations and a complete spiral curve, and continuous gradients of 1 in 25 in between. The ruling gradient is 1 in 40 for the next 90 miles, before the summit is reached at Maymyo (3,800ft). From here the line descends to cross the breathtaking viaduct over the Gokteik Gorge, 2,200ft in length and with its rail level 820ft above the river bed. This b/w printed card (Rowe & Co., Rangoon) shows a train crossing this engineering marvel around 1920. [79] Ceylon has a large (834 mile) broad gauge system supplemented by 117 miles of 2ft 6in gauge track. Several of the lines which serve the interior have all the classic characteristics of the mountain railway, the line from Polgahawela to Kandy and on to Bandulla reaching a summit of 6,226ft at Pattipola and including 20 miles of 1 in 44 on the section up to Kadungana, where banking engines were used. Commercial cards of the railway are scarce, this coloured card by the Colombo Apothecaries Co. dated 18 February 1908 is unusual in featuring a freight train.

Nº 24 Scene on Government Railway, Ceylon.

79

5060. *Tamalpais Tavern, Mt. Tamalpais, California, and Mt. Tamalpais Scenic Railway train.*

One of the earliest railroads built primarily for 'pleasure' purposes was the Mount Tamalpais Scenic Railway, a standard gauge line connecting Mill Valley, across the bay from San Francisco, with Mount Tamalpais summit (2,600ft). The railway's builders eschewed the use of rack rails and laid the line out to follow the contours of the hills, in a succession of curves that earned the line the soubriquet "the crookedest railway in the world." The railway featured 281 curves, including the 'double bow knot,' where the line paralleled itself five times in a few hundred feet. The line opened in 1896 and enjoyed a long period of prosperity before road competition, and a disastrous fire in 1929, led to abandonment in 1930. **[80]** At Mount Tamalpais summit the railroad erected the Tamalpais tavern, successive versions of which were destroyed in fires. The original building is shown here on a coloured card published by Cardinelli-Vincent Co., San Francisco, and posted in June 1911. **[81]** Hauling loads up steep grades by adhesion only demanded specialised motive power. Fortunately the demands of logging railroads in the US had already created a suitable design in the shape of the Shay and Heisler locomotive, where the drive was transmitted through gears, shown to good advantage here on a photographic card, probably an "official" published by the Railway.

13.
THE IRON STEED
MT. TAMALPAIS & MUIR WOODS RY.
CALIFORNIA

82

Colorado's Manitou and Pike's Peak Railroad had the distinction of being the highest scenic mountain railway in the world, reaching a height of 14,110ft asl. The line is standard gauge, 8.9 miles long, and uses the Abt rack system. Construction began in September 1889, and the whole line was completed in November 1890, although some trains to Half Way House had run during that summer. **[82]** The first locomotives were ordered from Baldwins and their specification required them to be able to push two cars weighing 21 tons up a grade of 1 in 4 at 3 mph. On this Detroit Photographic Co. coloured card, dated 1901 and posted in 1906, No. 3 is seen at work with one of the second generation coaches, the original four wheelers having proved impractical. **[83]** Modernisation came to the "Cog Road" in 1938 with the introduction of a single unit gasoline powered car, No. 7. This was a success and in the same year the railway ordered three more. No. 8, pictured here on a coloured card by Sanbourn Souvenir Co., Denver, is powered by three General Motors diesel engines and generates enough power to propel a trailer. The picture is taken at summit station, where an observation tower enabled passengers (on payment of 25c.) to enjoy even more spectacular views.

83

84

[84] The Mount Washington Cog Railway was the first successful scenic mountain railway, having opened in 1867. The 4ft 7^1/$_2$ in gauge line connected Marshfield Base Station (2,569ft) with Mount Washington summit (6,208ft) and was unusual insofar as much of the route was on wooden trestles built on the mountainside. At summit there was the usual restaurant and hotel. The style of lettering on the loco and tender dates this scene, depicted on a coloured card by Atlantic Post Card Co., to the 1931/35 period. [85] Mount Washington inspired a number of other lines, including the Green Mountain Railway, on Mount Desert Island, off the Maine coast. Opened in 1883, the railway conveyed tourists from sea level at Eagle Lake to a summit at 1,528ft, with the steepest grade 1 in 3. This view of No. 7 MOUNT DESERT at "the Gulch" gives a good view of the somewhat alarming looking design of the railway's infrastructure! The photo has been dated to 1883 so the card, published by Jordan Pond House, Seal Island, must have been published later, as picture postcards as such did not exist before about 1895. The railway was an early casualty of road competition, closing in 1911, but Loco No. 7 went on to a new life on the Mount Washington railway, becoming their No.4.

85

Dubbed "The Scenic Line of the World" the Denver and Rio Gande's extensive 3ft gauge network in Colorado comprised a 'main line' running west from Antonito through Chama to Durango, where it swung north to reach Silverton. Branches also served Farmington, Caliente (La Madera) and Pagosa Springs. At its peak the railway, including branches, comprised some 345 route miles and much of its route lay at 6,000ft asl and above. Operation was all year round despite the depredations of rockslides, washouts and the seasonal hazard of snow. Hit by road competition the network began to contract in 1932 and the last passenger services ran in 1951. However much of the route remained open to freight until 1968. **[86]** Commercial cards of "working" days are scarce, this example by Audio-Visual Design, New York, depicts locomotives 484 and 488 hauling snow removal equipment over Cumbres Pass in 1963. **[87]** Prompt action by lovers of the narrow gauge ensured the survival of two sections of the railway – from Durango to Silverton, and between Chama and Antonito. Passenger services operate over both sections, in summer only. This modern coloured card shows a train on Tanglefoot curve, east of Cumbres, in the early days of tourist operation. No. 483 is one of the successful K36 class introduced in 1925 and still in service at closure in 1968.

The building of the Canadian Pacific Railway was the foundation of modern Canada. After 20 years of surveys, carried out in the most arduous conditions in uncharted territory characterised by rockfalls, fallen trees, glacial torrents, and the danger of wild animals, construction of the transcontinental link began in earnest in 1879. Working from the eastern seaboard the engineers had first to conquer the dense forests and unhealthy swamplands of Southern Ontario, and the indian-infested prairies beyond. These problems however paled into insignificance compared to the challenge posed by the apparently impenetrable Rocky Mountains. To quote a contemporary source "Every mile of tunnel and track was sealed with the blood of men...there are bridges that hang in air – mere spider webs of iron...there are places where masonry is plastered, so to speak, against the solid rock of mountains. There are ledges halfway between heaven and earth, and elevations where the trains plunge headlong into clouds, and deep, cool ravines where the road-bed disputes with the darkness the realms of mysterious mountain torrents." Eventually the rails were driven through over a summit of 5,329ft at Kicking Horse Pass. The Selkirk range and Mount Sir Donald posed further obstacles, the former requiring the railway to climb to a summit of 4,300ft at Roger's Pass, the latter surmounted by boring a tunnel five miles in length, that took three years to build. Faced with these obstances it was a brilliant achievement for the lines from east and west to meet in 1885, and the first transcontinental trains ran in 1886. **[88]** One of the CPR's early schemes to improve the topography of the line (and so increase its capacity) was a realignment of the route between Kicking Horse Pass and the Yoho Valley, to eliminate the steep gradients which required four locomotives to haul a load of 700 tons. The new route, with gradients no steeper than 1 in 45, crossed the Kicking Horse River and, by means of two spiral tunnels (one 2,000ft in length) emerged the other side of Mount Stephen to regain the original line. The sheer grandeur of the scene is captured in this card by Valentine and Sons, Montreal and Toronto: the card carries the familiar JV logo and the publisher is presumably an overseas subsidiary of the legendary Dundee firm.

89

[89] Another view by Valentines of an unnamed location in the Rockies. The 'helper' engine is coupled part way through the train, to ease the load when the super-powered train runs over the many bridges and viaducts, a common North American practice. The line on the right is not a zig-zag but a 'trap' siding to catch runaways which might break away while negotiating the steep gradient ahead of our train. [90] Glacier station, named after the neighbouring Illecillewat Glacier, where the CPR built a large hotel complex to help attract visitors to the area. One of the railway's later improvement schemes involved re-routing of part of the line, eliminating seven complete circles, and a four mile section which despite the protection of snow-sheds was prone to blockages in winter. This isolated the old Glacier station $1^1/_2$ miles from the new railway, so a new road was driven through there, to enable visitors to reach the hotel complex. This is another card by Valentines, who seem to have had the monopoly on 'official' views of the CPR at this time.

C.P.R. Station, Glacier, Canadian Rockies

90

SELECT BIBLIOGRAPHY

Railways Through the Mountains of Europe – Ascanio Schneider   Ian Allan 1967
The Narrow Gauge Railways of Europe – Peter Allen and P. B. Whitehouse   Ian Allan 1959
Switzerland – its Railways and Cableways – Cecil J. Allen   Ian Allan 1967
Metre Gauge Railways in South and East Switzerland – John Marshall   David & Charles 1965
Far Wheels – Charles S. Small   Howell-North 1960
Austrian Travel Wonderland – W. J. K. Davies   Ian Allan 1974
French Minor Railways – W. J. K. Davies   David & Charles 1965
Mediterranean Island Railways – P. M. Kalla-Bishop   David & Charles 1970
Middle East Railways – Hugh Hughes   CRC 1981
The Snowdon Mountain Railway – Keith Turner   David & Charles 1973
The Snaefell Mountain Railway 1895-1970 – F. K. Pearson   LRTL 1971
Darjeeling and its Mountain Railway – A Guide and Souvenir – Darjeeling-Himalaya Railway Co.
Clouds on the Brienzer Rothorn – Peter Arnold   Plateway Press 1995
The Crookedest Railway in the World – T. Wurm & A. C. Graves   Howell-North 1960
The Pikes Peak Cog Road – Morris W. Abbott   Golden West Books 1972
Rio Grande Narrow Gauge – John B. Norwood   Heimburger House 1983
Railway to the Moon – Glen M. Kidder
Rack Railways of Australia – David Jehan   Author 1997
Railways of Latin America in Historic Postcards – Christopher Walker   Trackside Pubs. 1998
The Mont Cenis Fell Railway – P. J. G. Ransom   Twelveheads Press 1999
Swiss Mountain Railways Vol 1 – P. J. Kelley   Trackside Publications 1999
Rack Railroads and Models – Model Railroader   August 1976
Mountain Climbing Sans Rack – Modern Tramway   March-June 1979
The Railway Magazine – December 1952   March 1967
                           November 1967   May 1974
The Narrow Gauge – June 1966
Railway World – June 1960   March 1968
                July 1968   May 1971
                October 1971   November 1974
                November 1972   December 1972
                June 1973   September 1974
Railway Wonders of the World – various issues
Picture Postcard Monthly – various issues

INDEX TO RAILWAYS FEATURED